49 Polish Dessert Recipes for Home

By: Kelly Johnson

Table of Contents

- Pierogi with Sweet Cheese Filling
- Krówki (Polish Milk Caramels)
- Babka (Polish Easter Cake)
- Makowiec (Poppy Seed Roll)
- Pączki (Polish Doughnuts)
- Sernik (Polish Cheesecake)
- Piernik (Polish Gingerbread)
- Kremówka (Polish Cream Cake)
- Karpatka (Polish Carpathian Mountain Cake)
- Mazurek (Polish Easter Pastry)
- Ptasie Mleczko (Bird's Milk Cake)
- Kołaczki (Polish Fruit-filled Pastry)
- Kruszonka (Polish Crumb Cake)
- Torcik Wedlowski (Chocolate Wafer Cake)
- Kogel Mogel (Egg Yolk Dessert)
- Kluski Śląskie (Silesian Dumplings with Fruit)
- Kompot (Stewed Fruit Compote)
- Kisiel (Fruit Pudding)
- Jablecznik (Polish Apple Cake)
- Chałka (Polish Sweet Bread)
- Kokosanki (Coconut Cookies)
- Rogaliki (Rolled Jam-filled Cookies)
- Rurki z Kremem (Cream-filled Wafers)
- Miodownik (Honey Spice Cake)
- Faworki (Angel Wing Pastry)
- Zupa Nic (Rice Pudding with Fruit)
- Kruche Ciasto (Shortcrust Pastry)
- Paczki Drozdzowe (Yeasted Pastries)
- Placki Ziemniaczane (Potato Pancakes)
- Chłodnik (Cold Beet Soup)
- Kogel Mogel (Egg Yolk Dessert)
- Racuchy (Apple Pancakes)

Pierogi with Sweet Cheese Filling

Ingredients:

For the Dough:

- 2 cups all-purpose flour
- 1 large egg
- 1/2 teaspoon salt
- 1/2 cup sour cream
- 1/4 cup unsalted butter, melted
- Water (as needed)

For the Sweet Cheese Filling:

- 1 cup dry-curd farmer's cheese or ricotta cheese
- 1/4 cup granulated sugar
- 1 large egg yolk
- 1/2 teaspoon vanilla extract
- Zest of 1 lemon

Instructions:

For the Dough:

In a large bowl, whisk together the flour and salt.
In a separate bowl, mix the egg, sour cream, and melted butter until smooth. Gradually add the wet ingredients to the flour mixture, stirring until the dough comes together. If needed, add water, a tablespoon at a time, to form a soft dough.
Knead the dough on a lightly floured surface until smooth and elastic, about 5-7 minutes. Wrap the dough in plastic wrap and let it rest for 30 minutes.

For the Sweet Cheese Filling:

In a mixing bowl, combine the farmer's cheese (or ricotta), sugar, egg yolk, vanilla extract, and lemon zest. Mix until well combined and smooth. Set aside.

Assembling the Pierogi:

Roll out the dough on a floured surface to about 1/8-inch thickness.
Use a round cookie cutter (about 3 inches in diameter) to cut out circles of dough.

Place a small spoonful of the sweet cheese filling in the center of each dough circle.

Fold the dough over the filling to create a half-moon shape, pressing the edges together firmly to seal. You can crimp the edges with a fork for a decorative finish.

Repeat with the remaining dough and filling.

Cooking the Pierogi:

Bring a large pot of salted water to a boil.

Carefully drop the pierogi into the boiling water, a few at a time, and cook until they float to the surface (about 3-4 minutes).

Remove the cooked pierogi with a slotted spoon and transfer them to a plate.

Optionally, you can pan-fry the boiled pierogi in butter until golden and crispy.

Serving:

Serve the pierogi warm, either plain or with a dollop of sour cream, a sprinkle of powdered sugar, or a fruit compote.

Enjoy these delightful Pierogi with Sweet Cheese Filling as a sweet treat or dessert for any occasion!

Krówki (Polish Milk Caramels)

Ingredients:

- 1 cup granulated sugar
- 1 cup heavy cream
- 6 tablespoons unsalted butter, cut into pieces
- 1 teaspoon vanilla extract
- Pinch of salt

Instructions:

Prepare Ingredients:
- Before you start, have all your ingredients measured and ready to use. Line a baking dish or pan with parchment paper or foil, greased lightly with butter.

Cook the Sugar Mixture:
- In a heavy-bottomed saucepan, heat the sugar over medium heat, stirring constantly with a wooden spoon or silicone spatula. The sugar will start to melt and then turn amber in color.

Add Butter and Cream:
- Once the sugar has caramelized and turned golden brown, carefully add the butter, stirring continuously until it melts completely and combines with the sugar.

Stir in Cream and Vanilla:
- Slowly pour in the heavy cream while stirring constantly. Be cautious as the mixture may bubble vigorously. Continue stirring until everything is well combined and smooth.

Cook to Soft Ball Stage:
- Insert a candy thermometer into the mixture. Cook the caramel, stirring frequently, until it reaches the soft ball stage (about 240°F or 116°C). This stage ensures the caramel will set to the right consistency once cooled.

Remove from Heat:
- Once the caramel reaches the desired temperature, remove the saucepan from the heat and stir in the vanilla extract and a pinch of salt. Mix well.

Pour into Pan:
- Immediately pour the hot caramel mixture into the prepared baking dish. Allow it to cool for a few minutes.

Shape and Cut:
- Using a buttered knife or a bench scraper, begin cutting the caramel into small squares or rectangles while it's still warm. If the caramel becomes too hard to cut, you can warm the knife slightly under hot water.

Wrap Individually:
- Once the caramel pieces are cut, wrap each piece in small squares of waxed paper. Twist the ends to secure the wrapping.

Enjoy:

- Your homemade Krówki are ready to be enjoyed! Store them in an airtight container at room temperature for up to two weeks.

Krówki make wonderful gifts and are perfect for satisfying your sweet tooth. This homemade version captures the essence of these traditional Polish candies and can be customized with different flavors or additions like nuts or chocolate. Enjoy making and sharing these delightful milk caramels!

Babka (Polish Easter Cake)

Ingredients:

For the Dough:

- 3 cups all-purpose flour
- 1/2 cup granulated sugar
- 1 packet (2 1/4 teaspoons) instant yeast
- 1/2 teaspoon salt
- 3/4 cup warm milk (110°F - 115°F)
- 1/2 cup unsalted butter, softened
- 3 large eggs, at room temperature
- 1 teaspoon vanilla extract
- Zest of 1 lemon or orange

For the Filling (Optional):

- 1 cup raisins or chopped nuts (e.g., walnuts, pecans)
- 1/2 cup chocolate chips or chopped chocolate

For the Glaze:

- 1/2 cup powdered sugar
- 2-3 tablespoons milk
- 1/2 teaspoon vanilla extract

Instructions:

Activate the Yeast:
- In a small bowl, combine the warm milk and a pinch of sugar. Sprinkle the yeast over the milk, stir gently, and let it sit for about 5-10 minutes until foamy.

Mix the Dough:
- In a large mixing bowl or the bowl of a stand mixer fitted with a dough hook, combine the flour, sugar, and salt. Add the softened butter, eggs, vanilla extract, and citrus zest. Pour in the activated yeast mixture.
- Mix everything together until a soft dough forms. If using a stand mixer, knead the dough on medium speed for about 5-7 minutes until smooth and elastic. If kneading by hand, turn the dough out onto a lightly floured surface and knead for 10-12 minutes.

Rise the Dough:
- Place the dough in a greased bowl, cover with plastic wrap or a clean kitchen towel, and let it rise in a warm place for about 1-1.5 hours until doubled in size.

Prepare the Filling (Optional):
- If using, soak the raisins in warm water for about 10 minutes, then drain well. Combine the raisins, nuts, or chocolate chips in a bowl and set aside.

Shape the Babka:
- Once the dough has risen, punch it down gently to release the air. Turn it out onto a lightly floured surface and roll it into a rectangle, about 16x12 inches.
- Sprinkle the filling evenly over the dough, leaving a small border around the edges. Starting from one of the longer sides, roll the dough up tightly into a log.

Form the Cake:
- Grease a tall, cylindrical cake pan or a babka pan. Carefully transfer the rolled dough into the pan, tucking the ends underneath to form a ring or coil. Cover the pan loosely with plastic wrap and let it rise again for about 45 minutes to 1 hour.

Bake the Babka:
- Preheat the oven to 350°F (175°C). Once the babka has risen, bake it in the preheated oven for 30-35 minutes until golden brown and a skewer inserted into the center comes out clean.
- If the top starts to brown too quickly, cover loosely with foil during baking.

Cool and Glaze:
- Remove the babka from the oven and let it cool in the pan for 10-15 minutes. Carefully transfer the babka to a wire rack to cool completely.
- In a small bowl, whisk together the powdered sugar, milk, and vanilla extract to make the glaze. Drizzle the glaze over the cooled babka.

Serve:
- Slice the babka into pieces and serve. It's best enjoyed fresh but will keep well for a few days when stored in an airtight container at room temperature.

Enjoy this delightful Polish Easter babka with your family and friends during the holiday season!

You can customize the filling based on your preferences or keep it simple with just the buttery, sweet dough.

Makowiec (Poppy Seed Roll)

Ingredients:

For the Dough:

- 3 cups all-purpose flour
- 1/4 cup granulated sugar
- 1 packet (2 1/4 teaspoons) instant yeast
- 1/2 teaspoon salt
- 3/4 cup warm milk (110°F - 115°F)
- 1/4 cup unsalted butter, melted
- 2 large eggs

For the Poppy Seed Filling:

- 1 cup poppy seeds, ground
- 3/4 cup milk
- 1/2 cup granulated sugar
- 1/4 cup honey
- Zest of 1 lemon
- 1/2 cup raisins (optional)
- 1/4 cup chopped nuts (e.g., walnuts, almonds)

For Assembly:

- 1 egg, beaten (for egg wash)
- Powdered sugar, for dusting

Instructions:

Prepare the Dough:
- In a large mixing bowl or the bowl of a stand mixer fitted with a dough hook, combine the flour, sugar, yeast, and salt. Mix briefly to combine.
- In a separate bowl, whisk together the warm milk, melted butter, and eggs. Pour the wet ingredients into the dry ingredients and mix until a dough forms.
- Knead the dough for about 5-7 minutes until it becomes smooth and elastic. If using a stand mixer, knead on medium speed. If kneading by hand, turn the dough out onto a lightly floured surface.

First Rise:
- Place the dough in a greased bowl, cover with plastic wrap or a clean kitchen towel, and let it rise in a warm place for about 1-1.5 hours until doubled in size.

Prepare the Poppy Seed Filling:

- In a saucepan, combine the ground poppy seeds, milk, sugar, honey, and lemon zest. Cook over medium heat, stirring constantly, for about 10-15 minutes until the mixture thickens.
- Remove from heat and stir in the raisins and chopped nuts. Allow the filling to cool completely.

Assemble the Makowiec:
- Once the dough has risen, punch it down gently to release the air. Roll the dough out on a lightly floured surface into a rectangle, about 12x16 inches.
- Spread the cooled poppy seed filling evenly over the dough, leaving a small border around the edges. Starting from one of the longer sides, roll the dough up tightly into a log.

Second Rise:
- Place the rolled dough onto a parchment-lined baking sheet or into a greased baking dish. Cover loosely with plastic wrap or a clean kitchen towel and let it rise again for about 30-45 minutes.

Bake the Makowiec:
- Preheat the oven to 350°F (175°C). Brush the risen makowiec with beaten egg wash.
- Bake in the preheated oven for 30-35 minutes until golden brown and the internal temperature reaches 190°F (87°C).

Cool and Serve:
- Remove the makowiec from the oven and let it cool slightly. Dust with powdered sugar before slicing and serving.

Enjoy this delightful and flavorful Polish makowiec with a cup of coffee or tea. The combination of the soft, sweet dough and the rich poppy seed filling is truly irresistible! This recipe can be adapted with different variations of fillings or additional ingredients based on your preferences.

Pączki (Polish Doughnuts)

Ingredients:

For the Dough:

- 3 1/2 cups all-purpose flour
- 1/2 cup granulated sugar
- 1 packet (2 1/4 teaspoons) instant yeast
- 1/2 teaspoon salt
- 3/4 cup warm milk (110°F - 115°F)
- 3 tablespoons unsalted butter, melted
- 3 large egg yolks
- 1 teaspoon vanilla extract
- Zest of 1 lemon or orange

For Frying:

- Vegetable oil, for frying

For Filling:

- Your favorite jam or fruit preserves
- Powdered sugar, for dusting

Instructions:

Activate the Yeast:
- In a small bowl, combine the warm milk and a pinch of sugar. Sprinkle the yeast over the milk, stir gently, and let it sit for about 5-10 minutes until foamy.

Make the Dough:
- In a large mixing bowl or the bowl of a stand mixer fitted with a dough hook, combine the flour, sugar, and salt. Add the yeast mixture, melted butter, egg yolks, vanilla extract, and citrus zest.
- Mix everything together until a soft dough forms. If using a stand mixer, knead the dough on medium speed for about 5-7 minutes until smooth and elastic. If kneading by hand, turn the dough out onto a lightly floured surface and knead for 10-12 minutes.

First Rise:
- Place the dough in a greased bowl, cover with plastic wrap or a clean kitchen towel, and let it rise in a warm place for about 1-1.5 hours until doubled in size.

Shape the Doughnuts:

- Once the dough has risen, punch it down gently to release the air. Roll the dough out on a lightly floured surface to about 1/2 inch thickness.
- Using a round cookie cutter or a glass, cut out circles of dough. Place the dough circles on a parchment-lined baking sheet, cover with a clean kitchen towel, and let them rise again for about 30 minutes.

Fry the Pączki:
- Heat vegetable oil in a deep fryer or heavy-bottomed pot to 350°F (175°C). Carefully add a few doughnuts at a time to the hot oil, frying for about 2-3 minutes per side until golden brown and cooked through.
- Remove the fried doughnuts with a slotted spoon and drain on paper towels. Allow them to cool slightly.

Fill the Pączki:
- Once the doughnuts are cool enough to handle but still warm, use a piping bag fitted with a long nozzle to inject jam or fruit preserves into the center of each doughnut. You can also use a small knife to make a slit and spoon in the filling.

Dust with Powdered Sugar:
- Dust the filled pączki generously with powdered sugar while they are still warm.

Serve and Enjoy:
- Pączki are best enjoyed fresh on the day they are made. Serve them with coffee or tea for a delightful treat!

Make these delicious Polish doughnuts at home to celebrate special occasions or simply to indulge in a sweet and comforting treat. Customize the fillings with your favorite jams or even custard for variety!

Sernik (Polish Cheesecake)

Ingredients:

For the Crust:

- 1 1/2 cups graham cracker crumbs (about 10-12 graham crackers)
- 1/4 cup granulated sugar
- 1/2 cup unsalted butter, melted

For the Filling:

- 1 lb (450g) farmer's cheese (twaróg), well-drained and mashed or blended until smooth
- 1 lb (450g) cream cheese, softened at room temperature
- 1 1/4 cups granulated sugar
- 4 large eggs
- 1/4 cup all-purpose flour
- Zest of 1 lemon
- 1 teaspoon vanilla extract
- 1/2 cup sour cream

For Serving (Optional):

- Fresh berries or fruit compote
- Powdered sugar, for dusting

Instructions:

Preheat the Oven:
- Preheat your oven to 325°F (160°C). Grease a 9-inch springform pan and line the bottom with parchment paper.

Make the Crust:
- In a mixing bowl, combine the graham cracker crumbs, sugar, and melted butter. Mix until well combined and the mixture resembles wet sand.
- Press the crust mixture evenly into the bottom of the prepared springform pan. Use the back of a spoon or the bottom of a glass to compact the crust.

Prepare the Filling:

- In a large bowl or the bowl of a stand mixer, beat together the farmer's cheese, cream cheese, and granulated sugar until smooth and creamy.
- Add the eggs, one at a time, beating well after each addition. Scrape down the sides of the bowl as needed.
- Mix in the flour, lemon zest, vanilla extract, and sour cream until everything is well combined and smooth.

Assemble and Bake:

- Pour the cheesecake filling over the prepared crust in the springform pan. Smooth the top with a spatula.
- Place the springform pan on a baking sheet (to catch any potential drips) and bake in the preheated oven for about 60-70 minutes, or until the edges are set and the center is slightly jiggly.
- Turn off the oven and leave the cheesecake inside with the door slightly ajar for about 30 minutes to cool gradually.

Cool and Chill:

- Remove the cheesecake from the oven and let it cool completely at room temperature. Once cooled, refrigerate the cheesecake for at least 4 hours or overnight to set and firm up.

Serve:

- Before serving, run a knife around the edge of the springform pan to loosen the cheesecake. Carefully remove the sides of the pan.
- Optionally, top the sernik with fresh berries or a fruit compote before serving. Dust with powdered sugar if desired.

Enjoy this classic Polish sernik with its creamy texture and subtle tanginess. It's perfect for special occasions or as a delightful dessert any time of the year!

Piernik (Polish Gingerbread)

Ingredients:

For the Cake:

- 2 cups all-purpose flour
- 1 teaspoon baking soda
- 1 teaspoon baking powder
- 1 tablespoon ground cinnamon
- 1 teaspoon ground ginger
- 1/2 teaspoon ground cloves
- 1/2 teaspoon ground nutmeg
- 1/4 teaspoon ground allspice
- 1/4 teaspoon salt
- 1/2 cup unsalted butter, softened
- 1 cup granulated sugar
- 2 large eggs
- 1 cup honey
- 1 cup sour cream

For the Glaze (Optional):

- 1 cup powdered sugar
- 2-3 tablespoons milk
- 1/2 teaspoon vanilla extract

For Serving (Optional):

- Candied orange peel or chopped nuts for garnish

Instructions:

Preheat the Oven:
- Preheat your oven to 350°F (175°C). Grease and flour a 9x13-inch baking pan or line it with parchment paper.

Prepare the Dry Ingredients:
- In a medium bowl, whisk together the flour, baking soda, baking powder, ground spices (cinnamon, ginger, cloves, nutmeg, allspice), and salt. Set aside.

Cream the Butter and Sugar:
- In a large mixing bowl or the bowl of a stand mixer, cream together the softened butter and granulated sugar until light and fluffy.

Add Eggs and Honey:

- Beat in the eggs one at a time until well combined. Then add the honey and mix until smooth.

Alternate Mixing:
- Gradually add the dry flour mixture to the wet ingredients, alternating with the sour cream, beginning and ending with the flour mixture. Mix until just combined.

Bake the Piernik:
- Pour the batter into the prepared baking pan and spread it out evenly. Tap the pan gently on the countertop to remove any air bubbles.
- Bake in the preheated oven for 30-35 minutes, or until a toothpick inserted into the center comes out clean.

Cool the Cake:
- Allow the piernik to cool in the pan for about 10 minutes, then transfer it to a wire rack to cool completely.

Make the Glaze (Optional):
- In a small bowl, whisk together the powdered sugar, milk, and vanilla extract to make a smooth glaze. Adjust the consistency by adding more milk if needed.

Glaze and Serve:
- Once the piernik is completely cooled, drizzle the glaze over the top of the cake. Sprinkle with candied orange peel or chopped nuts if desired.
- Allow the glaze to set before slicing and serving the piernik.

Enjoy this delicious and fragrant Polish piernik with a cup of tea or coffee. It's a wonderful treat during the holiday season or any time you crave a spiced gingerbread cake!

Kremówka (Polish Cream Cake)

Ingredients:

For the Puff Pastry:

- 1 sheet (about 10x15 inches) store-bought puff pastry, thawed if frozen
- Granulated sugar, for sprinkling

For the Custard Filling:

- 2 cups whole milk
- 1/2 cup granulated sugar
- 1/4 cup cornstarch
- 4 large egg yolks
- 1 teaspoon vanilla extract
- 1 tablespoon unsalted butter

For the Whipped Cream Filling:

- 1 cup heavy cream, chilled
- 2 tablespoons powdered sugar
- 1 teaspoon vanilla extract

Instructions:

Prepare the Puff Pastry:
- Preheat your oven to 400°F (200°C). Line a baking sheet with parchment paper.
- Roll out the puff pastry sheet slightly to smooth out any creases. Transfer it to the prepared baking sheet.
- Prick the surface of the pastry with a fork to prevent it from puffing up too much during baking. Sprinkle the pastry evenly with granulated sugar.
- Bake in the preheated oven for 15-20 minutes or until the pastry is golden brown and crispy. Remove from the oven and let it cool completely on a wire rack.

Prepare the Custard Filling:
- In a saucepan, heat the milk over medium heat until it starts to simmer (do not boil).
- In a separate bowl, whisk together the sugar, cornstarch, and egg yolks until smooth and creamy.
- Gradually pour the hot milk into the egg mixture, whisking constantly to prevent the eggs from curdling.
- Return the mixture to the saucepan and cook over medium heat, stirring constantly, until the custard thickens and coats the back of a spoon.

- Remove from heat and stir in the vanilla extract and butter. Let the custard cool completely, covering the surface with plastic wrap to prevent a skin from forming.

Prepare the Whipped Cream Filling:
- In a mixing bowl, beat the chilled heavy cream, powdered sugar, and vanilla extract together until stiff peaks form.

Assemble the Kremówka:
- Once the puff pastry and custard are completely cooled, carefully cut the pastry sheet in half to create two equal rectangles.
- Spread the cooled custard evenly over one half of the pastry sheet.
- Spread the whipped cream evenly over the custard layer.
- Place the second half of the pastry sheet on top of the cream layer to create a sandwich.
- Refrigerate the assembled kremówka for at least 2 hours to allow the flavors to meld and the filling to set.

Serve:
- Before serving, dust the top of the kremówka with powdered sugar.
- Cut into squares or rectangles and serve chilled.

Enjoy this delightful Polish cream cake with its layers of flaky pastry and creamy filling. It's a perfect dessert for special occasions or anytime you want to treat yourself to a delicious homemade pastry!

Karpatka (Polish Carpathian Mountain Cake)

Ingredients:

For the Choux Pastry Layers:

- 1 cup water
- 1/2 cup unsalted butter
- 1 cup all-purpose flour
- 4 large eggs

For the Custard Filling:

- 4 cups whole milk
- 1 cup granulated sugar
- 1 cup all-purpose flour
- 6 large egg yolks
- 2 teaspoons vanilla extract
- 1 cup unsalted butter, softened

For Assembly:

- Powdered sugar, for dusting

Instructions:

Make the Choux Pastry Layers:
- Preheat your oven to 400°F (200°C). Line two baking sheets with parchment paper.
- In a medium saucepan, combine the water and butter. Bring to a boil over medium heat.
- Remove from heat and quickly stir in the flour until a smooth dough forms.
- Return the saucepan to low heat and cook the dough, stirring constantly, for about 1-2 minutes to slightly dry it out.
- Transfer the dough to a mixing bowl and let it cool slightly.
- Add the eggs, one at a time, mixing well after each addition until the dough is smooth and glossy.
- Divide the dough evenly between the two prepared baking sheets, spreading it into rectangles about 9x13 inches each.

- Bake in the preheated oven for 25-30 minutes or until golden brown and puffed. Remove from the oven and let the pastry layers cool completely on wire racks.

Make the Custard Filling:
- In a saucepan, heat the milk until steaming but not boiling.
- In a separate bowl, whisk together the sugar, flour, and egg yolks until smooth.
- Gradually pour the hot milk into the egg mixture, whisking constantly.
- Return the mixture to the saucepan and cook over medium heat, stirring constantly, until the custard thickens and coats the back of a spoon.
- Remove from heat and stir in the vanilla extract. Let the custard cool completely, covering the surface with plastic wrap to prevent a skin from forming.
- Once cooled, beat in the softened butter until smooth and creamy.

Assemble the Karpatka:
- Place one cooled choux pastry layer on a serving platter.
- Spread the custard filling evenly over the first layer.
- Top with the second choux pastry layer, pressing down gently to adhere.
- Refrigerate the assembled Karpatka for at least 2 hours to allow the flavors to meld and the filling to set.

Serve:
- Before serving, dust the top of the Karpatka with powdered sugar.
- Cut into squares or rectangles and serve chilled.

Enjoy this wonderful Polish Carpathian Mountain Cake with its light and airy choux pastry layers and creamy custard filling. It's sure to be a hit at any gathering or celebration!

Mazurek (Polish Easter Pastry)

Ingredients:

For the Shortcrust Pastry:

- 2 cups all-purpose flour
- 1/2 cup granulated sugar
- 1/2 teaspoon baking powder
- Pinch of salt
- 1/2 cup unsalted butter, cold and cut into small pieces
- 1 large egg
- 1 teaspoon vanilla extract

For the Topping:

- 1 cup ground almonds or walnuts
- 1/2 cup dried fruits (raisins, apricots, cranberries, etc.), chopped
- 1/2 cup fruit jam (apricot, raspberry, cherry, etc.)
- 1/2 cup chopped nuts (almonds, walnuts, hazelnuts, etc.)
- Zest of 1 lemon or orange
- 1/2 cup honey or caramel sauce (optional)
- Powdered sugar, for dusting

Instructions:

   Prepare the Shortcrust Pastry:
   - In a large mixing bowl, whisk together the flour, sugar, baking powder, and salt.
   - Add the cold butter pieces and use your fingers or a pastry cutter to rub the butter into the flour mixture until it resembles coarse crumbs.
   - Add the egg and vanilla extract to the mixture and knead gently until the dough comes together. Shape the dough into a ball, wrap it in plastic wrap, and refrigerate for at least 30 minutes.

   Preheat the Oven:
   - Preheat your oven to 350°F (175°C). Line a baking sheet with parchment paper.

   Roll Out the Dough:

- On a lightly floured surface, roll out the chilled dough into a rectangle or circle about 1/4 inch thick. Transfer the rolled-out dough onto the prepared baking sheet.

Prepare the Topping:
- In a bowl, combine the ground almonds or walnuts, chopped dried fruits, and lemon or orange zest.
- Spread the fruit jam evenly over the rolled-out dough, leaving a small border around the edges.
- Sprinkle the nut and fruit mixture over the jam layer, pressing it gently into the dough.

Bake the Mazurek:
- Bake in the preheated oven for 25-30 minutes or until the pastry is golden brown and cooked through.
- Remove from the oven and let the Mazurek cool completely on a wire rack.

Decorate and Serve:
- Once cooled, drizzle the Mazurek with honey or caramel sauce if desired.
- Sprinkle the Mazurek with powdered sugar before serving.
- Cut into squares or rectangles and serve as a delightful Easter treat.

Enjoy this delicious and festive Polish Mazurek with its delightful combination of flavors and textures. It's a wonderful addition to your Easter celebration or any special occasion!

Ptasie Mleczko (Bird's Milk Cake)

Ingredients:

For the Sponge Cake:

- 4 large eggs, at room temperature
- 1 cup granulated sugar
- 1 cup all-purpose flour
- 1 teaspoon baking powder
- Pinch of salt

For the Marshmallow Mousse:

- 1 cup granulated sugar
- 1/2 cup water
- 4 large egg whites, at room temperature
- 1 teaspoon vanilla extract
- 2 teaspoons gelatin powder
- 1/4 cup cold water
- 1 cup heavy cream, chilled

For the Chocolate Coating:

- 8 oz (about 225g) dark chocolate, chopped
- 1/4 cup unsalted butter

Instructions:

> Make the Sponge Cake:
> - Preheat your oven to 350°F (175°C). Grease and flour a 9x13-inch baking pan.
> - In a large mixing bowl, beat the eggs and sugar together until pale and fluffy.
> - In a separate bowl, sift together the flour, baking powder, and salt. Gradually fold the dry ingredients into the egg mixture until just combined.
> - Pour the batter into the prepared baking pan and spread it out evenly.
> - Bake in the preheated oven for 20-25 minutes or until a toothpick inserted into the center comes out clean.
> - Remove the cake from the oven and let it cool completely in the pan.

Make the Marshmallow Mousse:
- In a small bowl, sprinkle the gelatin over the cold water and let it bloom for about 5 minutes.
- In a saucepan, combine the sugar and 1/2 cup water. Cook over medium heat, stirring occasionally, until the sugar dissolves and the syrup reaches 240°F (115°C) on a candy thermometer.
- While the syrup is cooking, start whisking the egg whites in a clean mixing bowl until soft peaks form.
- Once the sugar syrup reaches the desired temperature, slowly pour it into the whipped egg whites while continuing to whisk. Add the bloomed gelatin and vanilla extract, and continue whisking until the mixture is thick and glossy.
- In a separate bowl, whip the chilled heavy cream until stiff peaks form.
- Gently fold the whipped cream into the marshmallow mixture until smooth and well combined.

Assemble the Ptasie Mleczko:
- Spread the marshmallow mousse evenly over the cooled sponge cake in the baking pan.
- Refrigerate the cake for at least 2 hours to set the mousse.

Make the Chocolate Coating:
- In a heatproof bowl set over a pot of simmering water (double boiler), melt the chopped dark chocolate and butter together until smooth.
- Remove the cake from the refrigerator and pour the melted chocolate mixture over the marshmallow mousse layer, spreading it out evenly with an offset spatula.

Chill and Serve:
- Return the cake to the refrigerator and chill for another 1-2 hours or until the chocolate coating is set.
- Once set, use a sharp knife to cut the Ptasie Mleczko into squares or rectangles.
- Serve and enjoy this delicious Polish dessert!

Ptasie Mleczko is a delightful and elegant dessert that's perfect for special occasions or gatherings. Its light and fluffy texture combined with the chocolate coating make it a favorite among dessert lovers. Enjoy making and sharing this wonderful treat with family and friends!

Kołaczki (Polish Fruit-filled Pastry)

Ingredients:

For the Pastry Dough:

- 2 cups all-purpose flour
- 1/2 teaspoon baking powder
- 1/4 teaspoon salt
- 1 cup unsalted butter, softened
- 8 oz cream cheese, softened
- 1/2 cup granulated sugar
- 1 teaspoon vanilla extract

For the Filling:

- Fruit preserves (apricot, raspberry, cherry, plum, etc.)
- Sweet cheese filling (optional; see notes below)
- Powdered sugar, for dusting

Instructions:

Make the Pastry Dough:
- In a bowl, whisk together the flour, baking powder, and salt. Set aside.
- In another bowl or using a stand mixer, beat together the softened butter, cream cheese, sugar, and vanilla extract until smooth and creamy.
- Gradually add the flour mixture to the butter mixture, mixing until a soft dough forms. Divide the dough into two equal portions, flatten each into a disk, wrap in plastic wrap, and refrigerate for at least 1 hour or until firm.

Prepare the Filling:
- If using sweet cheese filling, you can make it by combining farmer's cheese (twaróg), sugar, vanilla extract, and egg yolks until smooth. Adjust sweetness to taste.

Assemble and Bake:
- Preheat your oven to 350°F (175°C). Line baking sheets with parchment paper.
- On a lightly floured surface, roll out one portion of the chilled dough to about 1/8 inch thickness. Use a cookie cutter or a sharp knife to cut the dough into squares or circles (about 2-3 inches in size).

- Place a small spoonful of fruit preserves or sweet cheese filling in the center of each dough piece.
- Fold the corners or edges of the dough over the filling, pinching the dough slightly to seal and form a little envelope or pillow shape.
- Place the filled pastries on the prepared baking sheets, spacing them apart.
- Repeat with the remaining dough and filling.

Bake the Kołaczki:
- Bake in the preheated oven for 12-15 minutes or until the pastries are lightly golden.
- Remove from the oven and let the kołaczki cool on the baking sheets for a few minutes, then transfer to wire racks to cool completely.

Serve and Enjoy:
- Once cooled, dust the kołaczki with powdered sugar.
- Serve these delightful Polish pastries with a cup of tea or coffee.

Notes:

- Sweet Cheese Filling: To make sweet cheese filling, combine 8 oz of farmer's cheese (twaróg), 1/2 cup granulated sugar, 1 teaspoon vanilla extract, and 2 egg yolks until smooth. Adjust sweetness to taste.
- You can use any fruit preserves you like for the filling, such as apricot, raspberry, cherry, plum, or prune.

These homemade kołaczki are a wonderful addition to your dessert table and are sure to impress your family and friends. Enjoy making and savoring these delightful Polish pastries!

Kruszonka (Polish Crumb Cake)

Ingredients:

For the Cake Base:

- 2 cups all-purpose flour
- 1/2 cup granulated sugar
- 1 teaspoon baking powder
- 1/4 teaspoon salt
- 1/2 cup unsalted butter, softened
- 2 large eggs
- 1/4 cup sour cream or plain yogurt
- 1 teaspoon vanilla extract

For the Crumb Topping (Kruszonka):

- 1 cup all-purpose flour
- 3/4 cup granulated sugar
- 1/2 cup unsalted butter, melted

Optional Glaze:

- 1/2 cup powdered sugar
- 1-2 tablespoons milk
- 1/2 teaspoon vanilla extract

Instructions:

Preheat the Oven and Prepare the Pan:
- Preheat your oven to 350°F (175°C). Grease and flour a 9x9-inch baking pan or line it with parchment paper.

Make the Cake Base:
- In a mixing bowl, whisk together the flour, sugar, baking powder, and salt.
- Add the softened butter, eggs, sour cream or yogurt, and vanilla extract to the dry ingredients.
- Mix with a hand mixer or stand mixer until well combined and the batter is smooth.

Prepare the Crumb Topping (Kruszonka):
- In a separate bowl, combine the flour and sugar for the crumb topping.

- Pour the melted butter over the flour-sugar mixture and mix with a fork until coarse crumbs form. The mixture should resemble wet sand.

Assemble and Bake:
- Spread the cake batter evenly into the prepared baking pan, smoothing the top with a spatula.
- Sprinkle the crumb topping evenly over the cake batter, covering the entire surface.
- Gently press down on the crumb topping with your hands to help it adhere to the batter.

Bake the Kruszonka:
- Place the baking pan in the preheated oven and bake for 30-35 minutes, or until the top is golden brown and a toothpick inserted into the center comes out clean.

Optional Glaze (Icing):
- If desired, prepare the glaze by whisking together the powdered sugar, milk, and vanilla extract until smooth.
- Drizzle the glaze over the cooled kruszonka.

Serve and Enjoy:
- Allow the kruszonka to cool in the pan for about 15-20 minutes before slicing into squares.
- Serve warm or at room temperature, and enjoy this delicious Polish crumb cake with your favorite hot beverage.

Kruszonka is best enjoyed fresh and can be stored in an airtight container at room temperature for a few days. It's a simple yet delightful dessert that's sure to become a favorite in your home!

Torcik Wedlowski (Chocolate Wafer Cake)

Ingredients:

For the Chocolate Filling:

- 300g (10.5 oz) good quality dark chocolate, chopped
- 200g (7 oz) unsalted butter, softened
- 1 cup powdered sugar
- 1 teaspoon vanilla extract
- 2 tablespoons cocoa powder

For Assembly:

- 400g (14 oz) crispy wafer cookies (such as wafers or pirouette cookies)
- 1/2 cup strong brewed coffee or espresso, cooled
- Optional toppings: chocolate shavings, cocoa powder, whipped cream

Instructions:

Prepare the Chocolate Filling:
- In a heatproof bowl set over a pot of simmering water (double boiler), melt the chopped dark chocolate until smooth. Set aside to cool slightly.
- In a separate mixing bowl, beat the softened butter and powdered sugar together until light and fluffy.
- Add the melted chocolate, vanilla extract, and cocoa powder to the butter mixture. Beat until well combined and smooth. Set aside.

Assemble the Torcik Wedlowski:
- Line a rectangular loaf pan (about 9x5 inches) with parchment paper, leaving some overhang for easy removal later.
- Spread a thin layer of the chocolate filling on the bottom of the lined pan.
- Arrange a layer of crispy wafer cookies over the chocolate filling, breaking them into pieces to fit if needed.
- Lightly brush the wafer cookies with cooled brewed coffee or espresso.
- Spread a layer of chocolate filling over the wafer cookies, smoothing it out evenly.
- Continue layering with wafer cookies, coffee brushing, and chocolate filling until you've used up all the ingredients, finishing with a layer of chocolate filling on top.

Chill and Set:
- Cover the pan with plastic wrap and refrigerate the Torcik Wedlowski for at least 4-6 hours or overnight to allow it to set and firm up.

Serve:
- Once set, carefully lift the Torcik Wedlowski out of the pan using the parchment paper overhang.

- If desired, garnish the top with chocolate shavings, a dusting of cocoa powder, or whipped cream.
- Slice the cake into portions and serve chilled.

Enjoy this delightful Torcik Wedlowski with its layers of crispy wafer and creamy chocolate filling. It's a perfect dessert to impress your family and friends, especially for special occasions or gatherings. Store any leftovers in the refrigerator for several days. Each slice of this cake is a heavenly chocolate treat!

Kogel Mogel (Egg Yolk Dessert)

Ingredients:

- 4 large egg yolks
- 4-6 tablespoons granulated sugar (adjust to taste)
- 1/2 teaspoon vanilla extract (optional)
- Pinch of salt
- Optional toppings: whipped cream, fruit preserves, nuts, chocolate shavings

Instructions:

Prepare the Egg Yolks:
- Separate the egg yolks from the egg whites, ensuring there are no traces of egg whites in the yolks.

Mix the Egg Yolks and Sugar:
- In a heatproof bowl, whisk together the egg yolks, sugar, vanilla extract (if using), and a pinch of salt. Whisk vigorously until the mixture becomes pale and thick.

Cook the Mixture:
- Place the bowl over a pot of simmering water (double boiler method). Make sure the bottom of the bowl does not touch the water.
- Continue whisking the egg yolk mixture constantly over the simmering water. Cook until the mixture thickens to a custard-like consistency. This should take about 5-7 minutes.

Remove from Heat:
- Once the Kogel Mogel reaches the desired thickness (similar to a custard or pudding), remove the bowl from the heat.

Serve and Enjoy:
- Transfer the Kogel Mogel into serving dishes or small bowls.
- Serve warm or chilled, optionally topped with whipped cream, fruit preserves, nuts, or chocolate shavings.

Tips for Making Kogel Mogel:

- Consistency: The key to a good Kogel Mogel is achieving the right consistency. It should be thick and creamy but not too runny. Adjust the cooking time accordingly to achieve the desired texture.
- Sweetness: The amount of sugar can be adjusted based on your preference. Start with 4 tablespoons and add more if you prefer a sweeter dessert.

- Flavor Variations: You can customize the flavor of Kogel Mogel by adding different extracts such as almond extract or rum extract. Experiment with different toppings to create unique variations.

Kogel Mogel is a nostalgic and comforting dessert that's perfect for satisfying your sweet cravings. Enjoy this classic Polish treat as a delightful dessert or snack!

Kluski Śląskie (Silesian Dumplings with Fruit)

Ingredients:

For the Dumplings (Kluski Śląskie):

- 4 large starchy potatoes (such as Russet potatoes)
- 1 cup potato starch (or more as needed)
- 1 teaspoon salt
- 1 egg

For the Fruit Topping:

- 2 cups fresh or frozen mixed fruits (such as berries, cherries, or peaches)
- 1/4 cup granulated sugar (adjust to taste)
- 1 tablespoon cornstarch
- 1/4 cup water
- 1 teaspoon vanilla extract

Optional Toppings:

- Sour cream or whipped cream

Instructions:

> Prepare the Dumplings (Kluski Śląskie):
> - Peel and grate the potatoes using a box grater or a food processor.
> - Place the grated potatoes in a clean kitchen towel and squeeze out excess moisture over a bowl or sink.
> - Transfer the squeezed potatoes to a large mixing bowl. Add the potato starch, salt, and egg. Mix well with your hands until a smooth dough forms. The dough should be pliable and slightly sticky.
>
> Shape the Dumplings:
> - Bring a large pot of salted water to a boil.
> - Wet your hands with cold water to prevent sticking. Take a portion of the potato dough and shape it into a smooth oval dumpling, about the size of a small potato.
> - Gently drop the dumpling into the boiling water. Repeat with the remaining dough, working in batches to avoid overcrowding the pot.
> - Cook the dumplings in boiling water for about 8-10 minutes or until they float to the surface. Remove them with a slotted spoon and transfer to a colander to drain.
>
> Prepare the Fruit Topping:

- In a saucepan, combine the mixed fruits, sugar, and vanilla extract. Cook over medium heat until the fruits start to release their juices and become tender.
- In a small bowl, whisk together the cornstarch and water to make a slurry. Add the cornstarch mixture to the simmering fruits, stirring constantly.
- Continue cooking until the fruit mixture thickens into a syrupy consistency, about 2-3 minutes. Remove from heat.

Serve:
- Arrange the cooked Kluski Śląskie dumplings on serving plates.
- Spoon the warm fruit topping over the dumplings.
- Optionally, serve with a dollop of sour cream or whipped cream on top.
- Enjoy these delicious Kluski Śląskie dumplings with fruit as a sweet and comforting dessert!

Tips for Making Kluski Śląskie:

- Potatoes: Use starchy potatoes like Russet potatoes for the best texture. Ensure the grated potatoes are well-drained to prevent the dough from becoming too wet.
- Consistency: Adjust the amount of potato starch as needed to achieve a dough that is easy to handle and shape into dumplings.
- Fruit Topping: Feel free to use your favorite combination of fruits for the topping. Adjust the sweetness level by adding more or less sugar according to your taste preference.

Kluski Śląskie with fruit topping is a delightful and comforting dessert that showcases the traditional flavors of Polish cuisine. Enjoy this dish as a special treat for family gatherings or celebrations!

Kompot (Stewed Fruit Compote)

Ingredients:

- 4-5 cups mixed fresh or dried fruits (such as apples, pears, plums, cherries, berries)
- 8 cups water
- 1/2 cup granulated sugar (adjust to taste)
- 1 cinnamon stick (optional)
- 3-4 whole cloves (optional)
- Juice of 1 lemon (optional)

Instructions:

Prepare the Fruits:
- If using fresh fruits, wash them thoroughly. Peel and chop larger fruits like apples and pears into bite-sized pieces. Remove pits from stone fruits like plums or cherries.
- If using dried fruits, rinse them in cold water and drain.

Stew the Fruits:
- In a large pot, combine the prepared fruits with 8 cups of water.
- Add the sugar to the pot. If using spices like cinnamon stick and cloves, add them to the pot as well.
- Bring the mixture to a boil over medium-high heat.

Simmer:
- Once boiling, reduce the heat to low and let the mixture simmer gently for about 30-40 minutes or until the fruits are soft and tender.

Adjust Sweetness:
- Taste the kompot and adjust the sweetness by adding more sugar if needed. Keep in mind that the sweetness will slightly decrease when the kompot cools down.

Add Lemon Juice (Optional):
- If desired, add the juice of one lemon to the kompot for a touch of brightness and acidity. Stir well.

Serve:
- Remove the pot from the heat and let the kompot cool slightly.
- Serve the kompot warm by ladling it into cups or glasses. Alternatively, chill the kompot in the refrigerator for several hours before serving.

Storage:
- Store any leftover kompot in a sealed container in the refrigerator for up to 3-4 days. Enjoy it cold as a refreshing drink.

Tips for Making Kompot:

- Fruit Variations: Feel free to use a combination of your favorite fruits for the kompot. Popular choices include apples, pears, plums, cherries, berries, apricots, and raisins.

- Spices: Customize the flavor of your kompot by adding spices like cinnamon, cloves, or vanilla pods. These spices add warmth and depth to the beverage.
- Adjust Sweetness: The amount of sugar can be adjusted based on your preference and the natural sweetness of the fruits used. Start with a smaller amount and add more as needed.

Kompot is a versatile and comforting drink that can be enjoyed throughout the year, either warm during colder months or chilled as a refreshing summer beverage. It's a wonderful way to make use of seasonal fruits and create a naturally delicious drink for any occasion!

Kisiel (Fruit Pudding)

Ingredients:

- 1 cup fresh or frozen fruit (such as berries, cherries, apples)
- 3 cups water
- 4-6 tablespoons sugar (adjust to taste)
- 4 tablespoons potato starch or cornstarch
- Juice of 1 lemon (optional)
- Fresh fruit or whipped cream for serving (optional)

Instructions:

Prepare the Fruit:
- If using fresh fruit, wash and prepare them by removing pits, stems, or cores. If using apples, peel and chop them into small pieces.
- If using frozen fruit, thaw them slightly.

Cook the Fruit:
- In a medium saucepan, combine the fruit and water. Bring to a simmer over medium heat.
- Cook the fruit until it becomes soft and starts to break down, about 5-10 minutes depending on the type of fruit.

Sweeten the Mixture:
- Add sugar to the fruit mixture, stirring until dissolved. Adjust the amount of sugar based on the sweetness of the fruit and your preference.

Thicken with Starch:
- In a small bowl, mix the potato starch or cornstarch with a small amount of cold water to create a slurry (a smooth liquid mixture).
- Gradually pour the starch slurry into the simmering fruit mixture, stirring constantly.
- Continue to cook and stir until the mixture thickens and becomes glossy, similar to a pudding consistency. This should take about 2-3 minutes.

Add Lemon Juice (Optional):
- If desired, add the juice of one lemon to the kisiel for a touch of acidity and brightness. Stir well to combine.

Cool and Chill:
- Remove the saucepan from the heat and let the kisiel cool slightly.
- Pour the kisiel into serving bowls or glasses.
- Let the kisiel cool to room temperature, then cover and refrigerate until chilled and set, usually for at least 2-3 hours.

Serve:
- Serve the chilled kisiel on its own or garnish with fresh fruit or a dollop of whipped cream for added flavor and texture.

Tips for Making Kisiel:

- Fruit Variations: Experiment with different fruits to create unique flavors of kisiel. Berries, cherries, apples, and rhubarb are popular choices for this dessert.
- Consistency: Adjust the amount of starch to achieve your desired consistency. Add more starch for a thicker pudding-like texture or less for a lighter, jelly-like consistency.
- Sweetness: Taste the kisiel before chilling and adjust the sweetness by adding more sugar if needed.

Kisiel is a delightful and versatile dessert that can be enjoyed year-round. It's perfect for using seasonal fruits and makes a refreshing treat for any occasion. Serve this traditional Polish fruit pudding as a light and satisfying dessert after meals!

Jablecznik (Polish Apple Cake)

Ingredients:

For the Cake:

- 2 cups all-purpose flour
- 1 teaspoon baking powder
- 1/2 teaspoon baking soda
- 1/2 teaspoon ground cinnamon
- 1/4 teaspoon salt
- 1 cup granulated sugar
- 1/2 cup unsalted butter, softened
- 2 large eggs
- 1 teaspoon vanilla extract
- 1/2 cup sour cream or plain yogurt
- 3-4 medium-sized apples, peeled, cored, and thinly sliced

For the Streusel Topping:

- 1/2 cup all-purpose flour
- 1/4 cup granulated sugar
- 1/4 cup packed light brown sugar
- 1/2 teaspoon ground cinnamon
- 1/4 cup unsalted butter, melted

Optional Glaze:

- 1/2 cup powdered sugar
- 1-2 tablespoons milk or water
- 1/2 teaspoon vanilla extract

Instructions:

Preheat the Oven:
- Preheat your oven to 350°F (175°C). Grease and flour a 9x13-inch baking pan or line it with parchment paper for easy removal.

Make the Streusel Topping:
- In a small bowl, combine the flour, granulated sugar, brown sugar, and cinnamon for the streusel topping.
- Pour the melted butter over the dry ingredients and mix until crumbly. Set aside.

Prepare the Cake Batter:

- In a medium bowl, whisk together the flour, baking powder, baking soda, cinnamon, and salt. Set aside.
- In a large mixing bowl, cream together the softened butter and sugar until light and fluffy.
- Add the eggs, one at a time, beating well after each addition. Stir in the vanilla extract.
- Gradually add the dry flour mixture to the wet ingredients, alternating with the sour cream or yogurt, and mix until just combined.

Assemble the Cake:
- Spread half of the cake batter into the prepared baking pan, smoothing it out with a spatula.
- Arrange half of the sliced apples evenly over the batter.
- Sprinkle half of the streusel topping over the apples.
- Repeat with the remaining batter, apples, and streusel topping.

Bake the Cake:
- Bake in the preheated oven for 40-45 minutes or until the cake is golden brown and a toothpick inserted into the center comes out clean.

Optional Glaze:
- In a small bowl, whisk together the powdered sugar, milk or water, and vanilla extract until smooth.
- Drizzle the glaze over the cooled cake.

Serve and Enjoy:
- Allow the Jablecznik to cool in the pan for about 15-20 minutes before slicing into squares.
- Serve warm or at room temperature. Enjoy this delicious Polish Apple Cake with a cup of coffee or tea!

Tips for Making Jablecznik:

- Apple Varieties: Use your favorite baking apples such as Granny Smith, Honeycrisp, or Braeburn for the best flavor and texture in the cake.
- Storage: Store any leftover Jablecznik in an airtight container at room temperature for up to 2 days, or refrigerate for longer freshness.
- Variations: Feel free to add chopped nuts (such as walnuts or pecans) or dried fruits (such as raisins or cranberries) to the streusel topping for added crunch and flavor.

Jablecznik is a wonderful dessert that celebrates the sweetness of apples and the comfort of homemade baking. Enjoy this Polish Apple Cake with friends and family for a delightful treat!

Chałka (Polish Sweet Bread)

Ingredients:

For the Dough:

- 4 cups all-purpose flour, plus extra for dusting
- 1/2 cup granulated sugar
- 1 packet (2 1/4 teaspoons) active dry yeast
- 1 cup lukewarm water
- 3 large eggs, plus 1 egg for egg wash
- 1/4 cup vegetable oil or melted butter
- 1 teaspoon salt

For the Egg Wash:

- 1 egg yolk
- 1 tablespoon water

Optional Toppings:

- Sesame seeds or poppy seeds for sprinkling

Instructions:

Activate the Yeast:
- In a small bowl, dissolve 1 tablespoon of sugar in the lukewarm water. Sprinkle the yeast over the water and let it sit for about 5-10 minutes until foamy.

Prepare the Dough:
- In a large mixing bowl or the bowl of a stand mixer fitted with a dough hook, combine the flour, remaining sugar, and salt.
- Make a well in the center of the flour mixture and add the yeast mixture, 3 eggs, and vegetable oil or melted butter.
- Mix everything together until a dough forms.

Knead the Dough:
- Turn the dough out onto a floured surface and knead by hand for about 8-10 minutes until the dough is smooth and elastic. Alternatively, knead the dough using a stand mixer for about 5-7 minutes on medium speed.

First Rise:
- Place the dough in a lightly oiled bowl, cover with a clean kitchen towel or plastic wrap, and let it rise in a warm place for about 1-2 hours until doubled in size.

Shape the Chałka:

- After the dough has risen, punch it down to release the air and divide it into three equal portions.
- Roll each portion into a long rope about 14-16 inches long.
- Braid the ropes together to form a loaf, tucking the ends under the loaf.

Second Rise:
- Place the braided loaf on a baking sheet lined with parchment paper. Cover it loosely with a towel and let it rise again for about 30-45 minutes until slightly puffed.

Preheat the Oven:
- Meanwhile, preheat your oven to 375°F (190°C).

Egg Wash and Bake:
- In a small bowl, whisk together the egg yolk and water to make the egg wash.
- Brush the entire surface of the risen loaf with the egg wash.
- Optionally, sprinkle sesame seeds or poppy seeds over the top of the loaf.
- Bake the Chałka in the preheated oven for 25-30 minutes until golden brown and hollow-sounding when tapped on the bottom.

Cool and Serve:
- Allow the Chałka to cool on a wire rack before slicing.
- Serve slices of this delicious Polish sweet bread on its own, or enjoy it with butter and jam.

Tips for Making Chałka:

- Braiding: You can experiment with different braiding techniques to create decorative patterns with the dough.
- Variations: For a richer flavor, you can add raisins or chopped nuts to the dough before braiding.
- Storage: Store leftover Chałka in an airtight container or wrapped in plastic wrap at room temperature for up to 3-4 days. You can also freeze the bread for longer storage.

Chałka is a wonderful bread to enjoy for breakfast, brunch, or as a sweet treat any time of the day. Its soft and slightly sweet texture makes it a favorite among many cultures. Serve this homemade Polish sweet bread with pride and enjoy the delicious flavors!

Chałka (Polish Sweet Bread)

Ingredients:

For the Dough:

- 4 cups all-purpose flour, plus extra for dusting
- 1/2 cup granulated sugar
- 1 packet (2 1/4 teaspoons) active dry yeast
- 1 cup lukewarm water
- 3 large eggs, plus 1 egg for egg wash
- 1/4 cup vegetable oil or melted butter
- 1 teaspoon salt

For the Egg Wash:

- 1 egg yolk
- 1 tablespoon water

Optional Toppings:

- Sesame seeds or poppy seeds for sprinkling

Instructions:

Activate the Yeast:
- In a small bowl, dissolve 1 tablespoon of sugar in the lukewarm water. Sprinkle the yeast over the water and let it sit for about 5-10 minutes until foamy.

Prepare the Dough:
- In a large mixing bowl or the bowl of a stand mixer fitted with a dough hook, combine the flour, remaining sugar, and salt.
- Make a well in the center of the flour mixture and add the yeast mixture, 3 eggs, and vegetable oil or melted butter.
- Mix everything together until a dough forms.

Knead the Dough:
- Turn the dough out onto a floured surface and knead by hand for about 8-10 minutes until the dough is smooth and elastic. Alternatively, knead the dough using a stand mixer for about 5-7 minutes on medium speed.

First Rise:

- Place the dough in a lightly oiled bowl, cover with a clean kitchen towel or plastic wrap, and let it rise in a warm place for about 1-2 hours until doubled in size.

Shape the Chałka:
- After the dough has risen, punch it down to release the air and divide it into three equal portions.
- Roll each portion into a long rope about 14-16 inches long.
- Braid the ropes together to form a loaf, tucking the ends under the loaf.

Second Rise:
- Place the braided loaf on a baking sheet lined with parchment paper. Cover it loosely with a towel and let it rise again for about 30-45 minutes until slightly puffed.

Preheat the Oven:
- Meanwhile, preheat your oven to 375°F (190°C).

Egg Wash and Bake:
- In a small bowl, whisk together the egg yolk and water to make the egg wash.
- Brush the entire surface of the risen loaf with the egg wash.
- Optionally, sprinkle sesame seeds or poppy seeds over the top of the loaf.
- Bake the Chałka in the preheated oven for 25-30 minutes until golden brown and hollow-sounding when tapped on the bottom.

Cool and Serve:
- Allow the Chałka to cool on a wire rack before slicing.
- Serve slices of this delicious Polish sweet bread on its own, or enjoy it with butter and jam.

Tips for Making Chałka:

- Braiding: You can experiment with different braiding techniques to create decorative patterns with the dough.
- Variations: For a richer flavor, you can add raisins or chopped nuts to the dough before braiding.
- Storage: Store leftover Chałka in an airtight container or wrapped in plastic wrap at room temperature for up to 3-4 days. You can also freeze the bread for longer storage.

Chałka is a wonderful bread to enjoy for breakfast, brunch, or as a sweet treat any time of the day. Its soft and slightly sweet texture makes it a favorite among many cultures. Serve this homemade Polish sweet bread with pride and enjoy the delicious flavors!

Kokosanki (Coconut Cookies)

Ingredients:

- 200g (about 2 cups) unsweetened shredded coconut
- 200g (about 1 cup) granulated sugar
- 2 large eggs
- 1 teaspoon vanilla extract
- Pinch of salt

Optional Chocolate Drizzle (for decoration):

- 100g (about 1/2 cup) semi-sweet chocolate chips or chopped chocolate
- 1 teaspoon coconut oil or vegetable oil (to help with melting)

Instructions:

Preheat the Oven:
- Preheat your oven to 350°F (175°C). Line a baking sheet with parchment paper or silicone baking mat.

Mix the Ingredients:
- In a mixing bowl, combine the shredded coconut, granulated sugar, eggs, vanilla extract, and a pinch of salt.
- Mix everything together with a spoon or spatula until well combined and the mixture holds together.

Shape the Cookies:
- Take about 1 tablespoon of the coconut mixture and roll it into a ball using your hands.
- Place the coconut ball onto the prepared baking sheet. Repeat with the remaining mixture, spacing the cookies a few inches apart.

Bake the Cookies:
- Bake in the preheated oven for 12-15 minutes or until the edges of the cookies are golden brown.

Cool the Cookies:
- Remove the cookies from the oven and let them cool on the baking sheet for a few minutes.
- Transfer the cookies to a wire rack to cool completely.

Optional Chocolate Drizzle:

- If desired, melt the chocolate chips or chopped chocolate with the coconut oil in a heatproof bowl set over a pot of simmering water (double boiler method), stirring until smooth.
- Drizzle the melted chocolate over the cooled Kokosanki cookies using a spoon or fork.
- Let the chocolate set at room temperature or place the cookies in the refrigerator for a few minutes to speed up the process.

Serve and Enjoy:
- Once the chocolate is set, your Kokosanki coconut cookies are ready to enjoy!
- Store any leftover cookies in an airtight container at room temperature for up to one week.

Tips for Making Kokosanki:

- Coconut Texture: Use unsweetened shredded coconut for this recipe to control the sweetness. Sweetened coconut can make the cookies overly sweet.
- Cookie Size: You can adjust the size of the cookies based on your preference. Smaller cookies will bake faster, while larger cookies will take a bit longer.
- Chocolate Variation: If you prefer, you can dip the bottom of the Kokosanki cookies in melted chocolate instead of drizzling it on top.

Kokosanki are delightful coconut treats that are perfect for sharing with family and friends. They make a lovely addition to dessert platters or cookie trays for parties and gatherings. Enjoy these soft and chewy Polish coconut cookies with a cup of tea or coffee for a delightful treat!

Rogaliki (Rolled Jam-filled Cookies)

Ingredients:

For the Dough:

- 2 cups all-purpose flour
- 1 cup unsalted butter, cold and cubed
- 1/2 cup sour cream
- 1/4 cup granulated sugar
- 1 teaspoon vanilla extract
- 1/4 teaspoon salt

For Filling and Topping:

- 1/2 cup fruit jam or preserves (apricot, raspberry, plum, or your favorite flavor)
- Powdered sugar, for dusting

Instructions:

Prepare the Dough:
- In a large mixing bowl, combine the flour, granulated sugar, and salt.
- Add the cold cubed butter to the flour mixture. Using a pastry cutter or your fingers, work the butter into the flour until the mixture resembles coarse crumbs.

Add Sour Cream and Vanilla:
- Stir in the sour cream and vanilla extract to form a soft dough. Use your hands to bring the dough together into a ball.
- Wrap the dough in plastic wrap and refrigerate for at least 1 hour or until firm.

Preheat the Oven:
- Preheat your oven to 350°F (175°C). Line a baking sheet with parchment paper.

Roll out the Dough:
- On a lightly floured surface, roll out the chilled dough into a thin circle, about 1/8 inch thick.
- Use a round cookie cutter (about 3 inches in diameter) to cut out circles from the dough.

Fill and Shape the Rogaliki:
- Place a small teaspoon of fruit jam or preserves in the center of each dough circle.
- Fold the sides of each circle over the filling to form a crescent shape, pinching the edges together to seal. Alternatively, you can roll up each circle from one side to create a crescent shape.

Bake the Rogaliki:
- Place the shaped Rogaliki on the prepared baking sheet, leaving some space between each cookie.

- Bake in the preheated oven for 15-18 minutes or until the cookies are golden brown.

Cool and Dust with Powdered Sugar:
- Remove the baked Rogaliki from the oven and let them cool on the baking sheet for a few minutes.
- Transfer the cookies to a wire rack to cool completely.
- Dust the cooled Rogaliki with powdered sugar before serving.

Serve and Enjoy:
- Serve these delightful Rogaliki cookies with a cup of tea or coffee.
- Store any leftover cookies in an airtight container at room temperature for several days.

Tips for Making Rogaliki:

- Keep Dough Cold: It's important to keep the dough chilled throughout the process to prevent it from becoming too soft and sticky.
- Variations: Experiment with different flavors of fruit jam or preserves for the filling. Apricot, raspberry, plum, and strawberry are popular choices.
- Sealing the Edges: Ensure that the edges of the cookies are well-sealed to prevent the filling from leaking out during baking.

Rogaliki are a delightful treat that combines buttery, flaky pastry with sweet fruit filling. These rolled jam-filled cookies are perfect for holiday celebrations or afternoon tea. Enjoy making and sharing these traditional Polish cookies with your loved ones!

Rurki z Kremem (Cream-filled Wafers)

Ingredients:

For the Wafers (Rurki):

- 1 package of store-bought wafer tubes or rolls (available in specialty stores or online)
- Optional: melted chocolate for coating the ends of the wafers

For the Cream Filling:

- 1 cup heavy cream (cold)
- 1/4 cup powdered sugar (adjust to taste)
- 1 teaspoon vanilla extract
- Optional: cocoa powder or melted chocolate for chocolate-flavored cream

Instructions:

Prepare the Cream Filling:
- In a large mixing bowl, whip the cold heavy cream using a hand mixer or stand mixer until it begins to thicken.
- Gradually add the powdered sugar and vanilla extract to the whipped cream while continuing to beat. Beat until stiff peaks form and the cream is thick and holds its shape.
- If making chocolate-flavored cream, fold in cocoa powder or melted chocolate into the whipped cream until fully combined and smooth.

Fill the Wafer Tubes:
- Carefully fill each wafer tube with the prepared cream filling using a piping bag or a small spoon. Fill the tubes generously with the cream, making sure to evenly distribute the filling throughout the length of the tubes.

Optional Chocolate Coating:
- Dip each end of the filled wafer tubes into melted chocolate, if desired, to seal the ends and add a decorative touch. Allow the chocolate to set before serving.

Chill and Serve:
- Place the filled Rurki z Kremem in the refrigerator for at least 1 hour to allow the cream filling to set and the wafers to soften slightly.
- Serve chilled and enjoy these delightful cream-filled wafers as a sweet treat!

Tips for Making Rurki z Kremem:

- Variations: Experiment with different flavors for the cream filling by adding extracts such as almond, orange, or mint. You can also mix in crushed nuts or chocolate chips for added texture.

- Presentation: Decorate the filled wafers with a dusting of powdered sugar, sprinkles, or shaved chocolate for an elegant presentation.
- Storage: Keep the assembled Rurki z Kremem refrigerated in an airtight container to maintain freshness. Serve them chilled for the best taste and texture.

Rurki z Kremem are a delightful and elegant dessert that is perfect for special occasions or gatherings. Enjoy these cream-filled wafers as a delicious treat with family and friends, and customize them with your favorite flavors and decorations!

Miodownik (Honey Spice Cake)

Ingredients:

- 1 lb beef stew meat, cut into cubes (optional, for a meaty version)
- 1 large onion, finely chopped
- 2-3 garlic cloves, minced
- 2 carrots, peeled and diced
- 2 celery stalks, diced
- 1 large potato, peeled and diced
- 1 zucchini, diced
- 1/2 cup chopped fresh parsley
- 1/2 cup chopped fresh cilantro
- 2 tablespoons tomato paste
- 1 tablespoon hawaij spice mix (see recipe below)
- Salt and pepper, to taste
- Water or beef broth, as needed
- Cooked rice or pita bread, for serving

For the Hawaij Spice Mix:

- 1 tablespoon ground cumin
- 1 tablespoon ground black pepper
- 1 tablespoon ground turmeric
- 1 tablespoon ground coriander
- 1/2 tablespoon ground cardamom
- 1/2 tablespoon ground cloves
- 1/2 tablespoon ground cinnamon

Instructions:

Prepare the Hawaij Spice Mix:
- In a small bowl, combine all the spices (cumin, black pepper, turmeric, coriander, cardamom, cloves, cinnamon). Mix well and set aside.

Cook the Soup:
- In a large soup pot or Dutch oven, heat some oil over medium heat.
- If using beef stew meat, add it to the pot and brown on all sides. Remove the meat and set aside.
- Add chopped onion to the pot and sauté until translucent, about 5 minutes.
- Add minced garlic and sauté for another minute.

- Stir in diced carrots, celery, potato, and zucchini.

Add Spices and Tomato Paste:
- Sprinkle the hawaij spice mix over the vegetables and stir to coat evenly.
- Add tomato paste and mix well to incorporate.

Simmer the Soup:
- Return the browned meat (if using) to the pot.
- Pour in enough water or beef broth to cover the vegetables and meat.
- Bring the soup to a boil, then reduce the heat to low and let it simmer, partially covered, for about 1-1.5 hours until the meat is tender and the vegetables are cooked through.

Finish and Serve:
- Stir in chopped fresh parsley and cilantro.
- Season the soup with salt and pepper to taste.
- Serve the Yemenite soup hot, accompanied by cooked rice or torn pieces of pita bread.

Tips and Variations:

- Vegetarian Version: Omit the beef stew meat for a vegetarian version of Yemenite soup. You can add more vegetables or cooked chickpeas for protein.
- Spice Level: Adjust the amount of hawaij spice mix according to your preference for spiciness.
- Additional Flavors: Some variations of Yemenite soup include adding fenugreek leaves (methi) or fenugreek seeds for a distinct flavor.

Enjoy this flavorful and comforting Yemenite soup as a main course during Jewish holidays or any time you crave a warming and hearty dish. It's a wonderful representation of Yemeni culinary traditions and will surely delight your taste buds!

Faworki (Angel Wing Pastry)

Ingredients:

- 2 cups all-purpose flour
- 2 tablespoons granulated sugar
- 1/4 teaspoon salt
- 3 large egg yolks
- 2 tablespoons sour cream or plain yogurt
- 2 tablespoons unsalted butter, melted
- 1 teaspoon vanilla extract
- Vegetable oil, for frying
- Powdered sugar, for dusting

Instructions:

Prepare the Dough:
- In a large mixing bowl, whisk together the flour, sugar, and salt.
- In a separate bowl, whisk together the egg yolks, sour cream or yogurt, melted butter, and vanilla extract.

Combine Wet and Dry Ingredients:
- Gradually add the wet ingredients to the dry ingredients, mixing until a dough forms. Use your hands to knead the dough until smooth and elastic, about 5-7 minutes.

Rest the Dough:
- Wrap the dough in plastic wrap and let it rest at room temperature for at least 30 minutes, or up to 1 hour.

Roll and Cut the Dough:
- On a lightly floured surface, roll out the dough thinly (about 1/8 inch thick).
- Use a sharp knife or pastry cutter to cut the dough into strips, about 1 inch wide and 4-5 inches long. You can also use a fluted pastry wheel for a decorative edge.

Form the Angel Wings:
- Make a small slit in the center of each dough strip.
- Pull one end of the dough strip through the slit to create a twist or bow-like shape.

Fry the Faworki:
- In a deep skillet or pot, heat vegetable oil to 350°F (175°C) over medium heat.
- Carefully add a few faworki at a time to the hot oil, frying until golden brown and crispy, about 1-2 minutes per side.
- Use a slotted spoon to transfer the fried faworki to a paper towel-lined plate to drain excess oil. Allow them to cool slightly.

Dust with Powdered Sugar:

- Generously dust the warm faworki with powdered sugar while they are still slightly warm. Alternatively, you can place the faworki in a paper bag with powdered sugar and shake to coat.

Serve and Enjoy:
- Serve the faworki (angel wing pastries) as a delightful sweet treat during Jewish holidays or festive occasions.
- Store any leftover faworki in an airtight container at room temperature for up to several days.

Tips and Variations:

- Flavor Variations: Add a pinch of ground cinnamon or lemon zest to the dough for extra flavor.
- Decoration: You can drizzle melted chocolate or sprinkle colored sprinkles over the powdered sugar for a festive touch.
- Make-Ahead: Prepare the dough in advance and store it in the refrigerator until ready to roll and fry.

Enjoy making and indulging in these crispy and sweet faworki (angel wing pastries) as a delightful addition to your holiday celebrations or special gatherings. They are sure to be a hit with family and friends!

Zupa Nic (Rice Pudding with Fruit)

Ingredients:

- 1/2 cup white rice (short-grain or medium-grain)
- 6 cups water
- 1/2 cup dried mixed fruits (such as raisins, prunes, apricots, apples)
- 1 cinnamon stick
- 1/4 cup granulated sugar (adjust to taste)
- 1 teaspoon vanilla extract
- Juice of 1 lemon
- Fresh fruit slices (optional, for garnish)
- Ground cinnamon or nutmeg, for sprinkling (optional)

Instructions:

Cook the Rice:
- In a large pot, bring 6 cups of water to a boil.
- Add the white rice to the boiling water and cook until the rice is tender, about 15-20 minutes.
- Drain the cooked rice and set it aside.

Prepare the Fruit Soup:
- In the same pot (or a clean pot), combine the cooked rice, dried mixed fruits, and cinnamon stick.
- Add enough water to cover the ingredients (about 6 cups) and bring to a simmer over medium heat.

Sweeten and Flavor the Soup:
- Stir in granulated sugar and vanilla extract into the soup.
- Continue to simmer the soup for another 10-15 minutes, or until the dried fruits are softened and the flavors are well combined.
- Adjust sweetness with more sugar, if desired.

Finish and Serve:
- Remove the cinnamon stick from the soup.
- Stir in the lemon juice to brighten the flavors.
- Ladle the fruit soup into serving bowls.
- Garnish with fresh fruit slices (such as orange segments or berries) if desired.
- Sprinkle ground cinnamon or nutmeg over the top for added flavor.

Chill and Enjoy:

- Serve the rice pudding fruit soup warm or chilled, depending on your preference.
- Store any leftover soup in the refrigerator and enjoy it within a few days.

Tips and Variations:

- Creamy Option: For a creamier texture, you can stir in a splash of heavy cream or coconut milk into the soup just before serving.
- Additional Flavors: Feel free to experiment with different dried fruits such as cranberries, cherries, or figs to customize the soup to your liking.
- Make-Ahead: This soup can be made ahead of time and stored in the refrigerator. The flavors often improve after sitting overnight.

This rice pudding fruit soup (zupa nic) is a comforting and delightful dessert soup that is perfect for special occasions or holiday gatherings. It's a sweet treat that can be enjoyed warm or chilled, and it's sure to be a memorable addition to your festive menu!

Kruche Ciasto (Shortcrust Pastry)

Ingredients:

- 2 cups all-purpose flour
- 1/2 cup granulated sugar
- 1/4 teaspoon salt
- 1 cup unsalted butter, cold and cubed
- 1 large egg
- 1-2 tablespoons cold water (as needed)

Instructions:

  Prepare the Dough:
  - In a large mixing bowl, whisk together the flour, sugar, and salt.
  - Add the cold, cubed butter to the flour mixture.
  - Use a pastry cutter or fork to cut the butter into the flour until the mixture resembles coarse crumbs. The butter should be well distributed but still visible.

  Add the Egg:
  - In a small bowl, lightly beat the egg.
  - Drizzle the beaten egg over the flour-butter mixture.

  Mix the Dough:
  - Gently stir the mixture with a fork or pastry blender until the dough starts to come together.
  - If the dough seems too dry or crumbly, add cold water, 1 tablespoon at a time, and continue mixing until the dough forms a cohesive ball. Be careful not to overwork the dough.

  Chill the Dough (Optional):
  - Shape the dough into a disk and wrap it in plastic wrap.
  - Chill the dough in the refrigerator for at least 30 minutes (or up to 24 hours) to allow the butter to firm up and the dough to rest.

  Roll Out the Dough:
  - On a lightly floured surface, roll out the chilled dough into a circle of desired thickness, depending on your recipe.
  - Use the rolled-out dough to line a pie dish or tart pan, or use cookie cutters to create shapes for cookies or pastries.

  Bake or Use as Directed:
  - Follow the specific recipe instructions for baking or using the shortcrust pastry in your desired dish (e.g., pie, tart, cookies).
  - If pre-baking the crust (blind baking), preheat the oven to 375°F (190°C) and bake the crust for about 15-20 minutes until lightly golden.

Tips and Variations:

- Flavor Variations: Add vanilla extract or citrus zest to the dough for extra flavor.

- Sweet or Savory: Adjust the amount of sugar or salt based on whether you're making a sweet or savory dish.
- Handling the Dough: Work quickly and avoid overmixing the dough to prevent developing too much gluten, which can make the pastry tough.
- Storage: Store unused dough in the refrigerator for a few days or freeze it for longer storage. Thaw frozen dough in the refrigerator before using.

This kruche ciasto (shortcrust pastry) recipe is a basic and essential dough that can be used in a wide variety of recipes. Whether you're making a fruit tart, savory quiche, or simple cookies, this buttery and tender pastry dough will elevate your homemade creations!

Paczki Drozdzowe (Yeasted Pastries)

Ingredients:

For the Dough:

- 2 1/4 teaspoons (1 packet) active dry yeast
- 1/4 cup granulated sugar
- 3/4 cup lukewarm milk
- 3 1/2 cups all-purpose flour
- 1/2 teaspoon salt
- 3 large egg yolks
- 1/4 cup unsalted butter, softened
- 1 teaspoon vanilla extract
- Zest of 1 lemon or orange

For Frying and Filling:

- Vegetable oil, for frying
- Fruit jam or preserves (such as raspberry, plum, or rose hip)
- Powdered sugar, for dusting

Instructions:

Activate the Yeast:
- In a small bowl, dissolve the yeast and 1 tablespoon of sugar in lukewarm milk. Let it sit for about 5-10 minutes until foamy.

Prepare the Dough:
- In a large mixing bowl, combine the flour, remaining sugar, and salt.
- Make a well in the center of the dry ingredients and add the yeast mixture, egg yolks, softened butter, vanilla extract, and citrus zest.
- Mix the ingredients together to form a soft dough.

Knead the Dough:
- Turn the dough out onto a lightly floured surface and knead for about 5-7 minutes until smooth and elastic. Alternatively, use a stand mixer with a dough hook attachment.

First Rise:
- Place the dough in a greased bowl, cover with a clean kitchen towel, and let it rise in a warm place for about 1-1.5 hours until doubled in size.

Shape and Fill the Pączki:

- Punch down the risen dough and roll it out on a lightly floured surface to about 1/2 inch thickness.
- Use a round cookie cutter or glass to cut out circles of dough (about 3 inches in diameter).
- Place a teaspoon of fruit jam in the center of each dough circle.
- Fold the dough over the filling and pinch the edges to seal, forming a ball-shaped pastry.

Second Rise:
- Place the filled pastries on a parchment-lined baking sheet, cover with a towel, and let them rise for another 30-45 minutes until puffy.

Fry the Pączki:
- In a deep pot or fryer, heat vegetable oil to 350°F (175°C).
- Carefully add a few pączki at a time to the hot oil and fry for about 2-3 minutes per side until golden brown.
- Remove the fried pastries with a slotted spoon and drain on paper towels.

Finish and Serve:
- Dust the warm pączki with powdered sugar while they are still slightly warm.
- Serve the yeasted pastries fresh and enjoy!

Tips and Variations:

- Filling Ideas: Besides fruit jam, you can use pastry cream, Nutella, or lemon curd as fillings for pączki.
- Flavor Variations: Add ground cinnamon or cardamom to the dough for extra flavor.
- Baking Option: If you prefer a baked version, you can place the filled pastries on a baking sheet, brush with egg wash, and bake at 375°F (190°C) for 12-15 minutes until golden brown.

These pączki drożdżowe are a delightful and indulgent treat, perfect for celebrating special occasions or enjoying as a sweet snack. The soft, pillowy texture and fruity filling make them irresistible!

Placki Ziemniaczane (Potato Pancakes)

Ingredients:

- 4 large russet potatoes (about 2 pounds), peeled
- 1 small onion, finely grated or minced
- 2 large eggs, lightly beaten
- 3-4 tablespoons all-purpose flour
- 1 teaspoon salt, or to taste
- 1/2 teaspoon black pepper
- Vegetable oil, for frying
- Sour cream or applesauce, for serving (optional)
- Chopped fresh chives or parsley, for garnish (optional)

Instructions:

- Grate the Potatoes:
    - Using a box grater or a food processor fitted with a grating disc, grate the peeled potatoes. Place the grated potatoes in a clean kitchen towel and squeeze out as much liquid as possible. Transfer the squeezed potatoes to a large mixing bowl.
- Prepare the Batter:
    - Add finely grated or minced onion, beaten eggs, flour, salt, and black pepper to the bowl with the grated potatoes. Mix well until all ingredients are combined.
- Heat the Oil:
    - In a large skillet or frying pan, heat enough vegetable oil over medium-high heat to generously coat the bottom of the pan.
- Fry the Potato Pancakes:
    - Once the oil is hot, drop spoonfuls of the potato batter into the skillet, flattening them slightly with the back of a spoon to form pancakes (about 3-4 inches in diameter).
    - Fry the pancakes for 3-4 minutes on each side, or until golden brown and crispy. Adjust the heat as needed to prevent burning.
- Drain and Serve:
    - Remove the cooked potato pancakes from the skillet and drain them on paper towels to remove excess oil.
    - Keep the pancakes warm in a low oven while you fry the remaining batter.
- Serve and Garnish:

- Serve the placki ziemniaczane hot with sour cream or applesauce on the side.
- Garnish with chopped fresh chives or parsley if desired.

Tips and Variations:

- Variations: Add grated garlic or chopped fresh herbs (such as dill or parsley) to the potato batter for extra flavor.
- Crispy Tips: For extra crispy potato pancakes, make sure to squeeze out as much moisture as possible from the grated potatoes before mixing with other ingredients.
- Make-Ahead: You can prepare the potato batter in advance and fry the pancakes just before serving. Store the batter in the refrigerator and mix well before frying.

These placki ziemniaczane (potato pancakes) are delicious as a side dish or appetizer, especially during holiday gatherings or family meals. They are best enjoyed fresh and hot, straight from the frying pan! Serve them with your favorite toppings and enjoy the crispy, savory goodness of these traditional Polish potato pancakes.

Chłodnik (Cold Beet Soup)

Ingredients:

- 3 medium beets, cooked and peeled
- 1 cucumber, peeled and diced
- 4 radishes, diced
- 2 scallions, finely chopped
- 2 cups buttermilk or kefir
- 1 cup sour cream
- 1 tablespoon fresh dill, chopped
- 1 tablespoon fresh parsley, chopped
- 1 tablespoon fresh chives, chopped
- 1 tablespoon white wine vinegar or lemon juice
- 1-2 teaspoons sugar, or to taste
- Salt and pepper, to taste
- Hard-boiled eggs, sliced (for garnish, optional)

Instructions:

Prepare the Beets:
- Cook the beets by boiling or roasting them until tender. Once cooked, allow them to cool, then peel and dice them.

Combine Ingredients:
- In a large mixing bowl, combine the diced beets, cucumber, radishes, and chopped scallions.

Mix the Soup Base:
- In another bowl, whisk together the buttermilk (or kefir) and sour cream until smooth.
- Add the chopped dill, parsley, chives, white wine vinegar (or lemon juice), sugar, salt, and pepper to the buttermilk mixture. Mix well to combine.

Combine and Chill:
- Pour the buttermilk mixture over the diced vegetables in the large bowl.
- Stir gently to combine all the ingredients.
- Taste and adjust seasoning with more salt, pepper, or sugar if needed.
- Cover the bowl and refrigerate the soup for at least 2 hours to chill and allow the flavors to meld.

Serve and Garnish:
- Stir the chilled soup before serving.
- Ladle the chłodnik into bowls.
- Garnish each serving with sliced hard-boiled eggs (if using) and additional chopped fresh herbs.
- Serve the cold beet soup with crusty bread or rye bread on the side.

Tips and Variations:

- Vegetarian Variation: Use vegetable broth or water instead of buttermilk for a dairy-free version.
- Creamy Texture: For a smoother texture, blend some of the soup mixture in a blender or food processor before adding it back to the diced vegetables.
- Additional Ingredients: Some variations of chłodnik include adding boiled potatoes, diced apples, or cooked pearl barley for extra texture and flavor.

This chłodnik (cold beet soup) is a wonderful dish to enjoy during warm weather, as it's both cooling and nutritious. The combination of earthy beets, crunchy vegetables, and creamy buttermilk creates a delightful and refreshing soup that is perfect for summer meals or as part of a festive spread. Enjoy this traditional Polish dish and savor its unique flavors!

Kogel Mogel (Egg Yolk Dessert)

Ingredients:

- 4 large egg yolks
- 4 tablespoons granulated sugar (adjust to taste)
- 1 teaspoon vanilla extract or other flavorings (optional)
- Ground cinnamon or grated chocolate, for garnish (optional)

Instructions:

Prepare the Egg Yolks:
- Separate the egg yolks from the egg whites and place the yolks in a mixing bowl.

Whip the Egg Yolks:
- Using a hand mixer or whisk, beat the egg yolks until they become pale and fluffy.

Add Sugar and Flavoring:
- Gradually add the sugar to the whipped egg yolks while continuing to beat.
- Mix in the vanilla extract or any other flavorings you prefer, such as almond extract or rum (if using).

Continue Beating:
- Keep beating the mixture until it becomes thick and creamy, with a texture similar to softly whipped cream.

Serve and Garnish:
- Transfer the whipped egg yolk mixture into serving dishes or small dessert bowls.
- Optionally, sprinkle some ground cinnamon or grated chocolate on top for garnish.

Enjoy Kogel Mogel:
- Serve the Kogel Mogel immediately as a simple and delicious dessert.

Tips and Variations:

- Flavor Variations: Experiment with different flavorings such as citrus zest (lemon or orange), coffee extract, or a dash of liqueur for added depth of flavor.
- Texture Adjustment: Depending on your preference, you can adjust the sweetness by adding more or less sugar. You can also vary the texture by beating the egg yolks for a shorter or longer time.
- Serving Suggestions: Kogel Mogel can be enjoyed on its own as a sweet and creamy dessert. It can also be used as a topping for cakes, pancakes, or ice cream.

Kogel Mogel is a nostalgic dessert that brings back memories of homemade treats. Its simplicity and rich flavor make it a delightful dessert option, especially for those who appreciate the taste of eggs and sugar. Try this traditional Polish recipe and enjoy the creamy goodness of Kogel Mogel!

Racuchy (Apple Pancakes)

Ingredients:

- 2 large apples (such as Granny Smith), peeled and diced
- 1 cup all-purpose flour
- 1 tablespoon granulated sugar
- 1 teaspoon baking powder
- 1/4 teaspoon salt
- 1 teaspoon ground cinnamon
- 2/3 cup milk
- 1 large egg
- 1 teaspoon vanilla extract
- Butter or oil, for cooking
- Powdered sugar, for dusting (optional)
- Maple syrup or honey, for serving (optional)

Instructions:

Prepare the Apples:
- Peel and dice the apples into small pieces. Set aside.

Make the Pancake Batter:
- In a mixing bowl, whisk together the flour, sugar, baking powder, salt, and ground cinnamon.

Combine Wet Ingredients:
- In another bowl, whisk together the milk, egg, and vanilla extract until well combined.

Mix Batter:
- Pour the wet ingredients into the dry ingredients and mix until just combined. Do not overmix; the batter may be slightly lumpy.

Fold in Apples:
- Gently fold the diced apples into the pancake batter, ensuring they are evenly distributed.

Cook the Pancakes:
- Heat a non-stick skillet or griddle over medium heat and add a small amount of butter or oil.
- Spoon about 1/4 cup of batter onto the skillet for each pancake, spreading it slightly into a round shape.

Cook Until Golden:

- Cook the pancakes for about 2-3 minutes on the first side, or until bubbles form on the surface and the edges look set.
- Flip the pancakes and cook for another 1-2 minutes on the second side, or until golden brown and cooked through.

Serve and Enjoy:
- Transfer the cooked racuchy to a plate.
- Dust with powdered sugar if desired.
- Serve warm with maple syrup, honey, or your favorite pancake toppings.

Tips and Variations:

- Additional Flavors: Feel free to add a pinch of nutmeg or cardamom to the batter for extra flavor.
- Texture: For a lighter texture, you can separate the egg, beat the egg white until stiff peaks form, and fold it into the batter just before cooking.
- Apple Varieties: Experiment with different types of apples for varying levels of sweetness and tartness.

Racuchy are best enjoyed warm and fresh, straight from the skillet. They make a delightful breakfast or brunch dish, especially during apple season when apples are at their peak. Give this recipe a try and savor the delicious combination of apples and cinnamon in these Polish-style apple pancakes!

www.ingramcontent.com/pod-product-compliance
Lightning Source LLC
LaVergne TN
LVHW081619060526
838201LV00054B/2320